How the Ear Can Hear

Written by Kate Scott

Collins

Ears are terrific.

Stamp!

Splat!

They help us to hear.

Scrunch!

Crack!

3

Ears keep you alert.

You can still hear if you rest or nap.

This is what the parts of an ear look like.

ear

ear canal

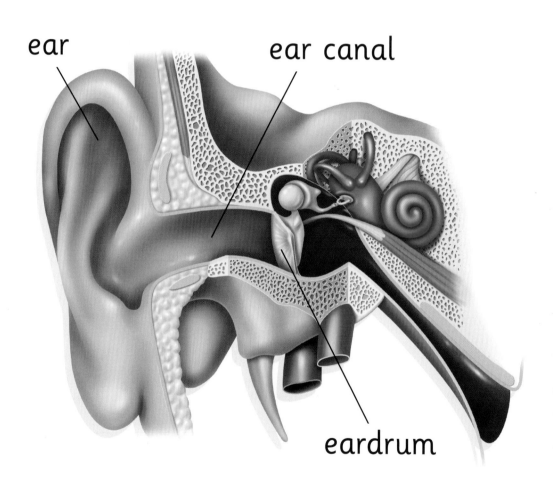

eardrum

Do not stick objects in ears.
You might hurt them!

The little hairs deep in ears help us to hear.

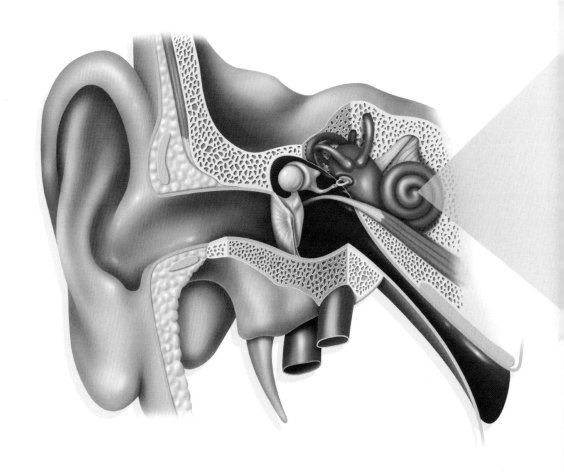

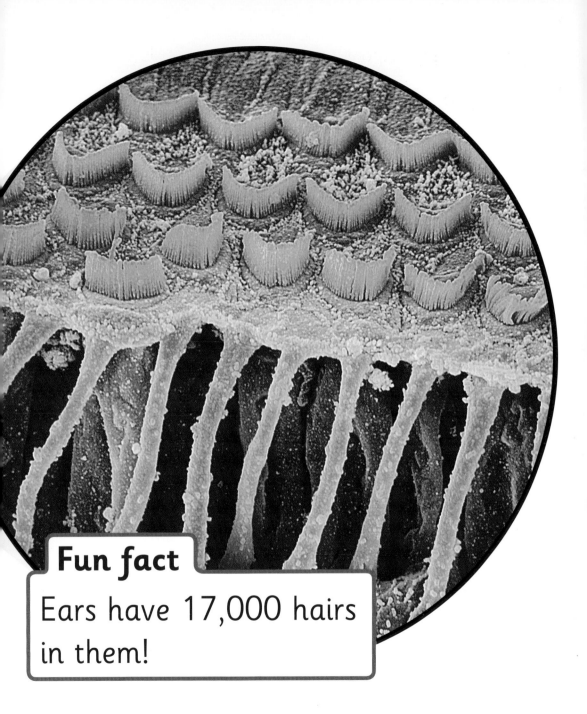

Fun fact

Ears have 17,000 hairs in them!

Wax keeps dust out of ears.

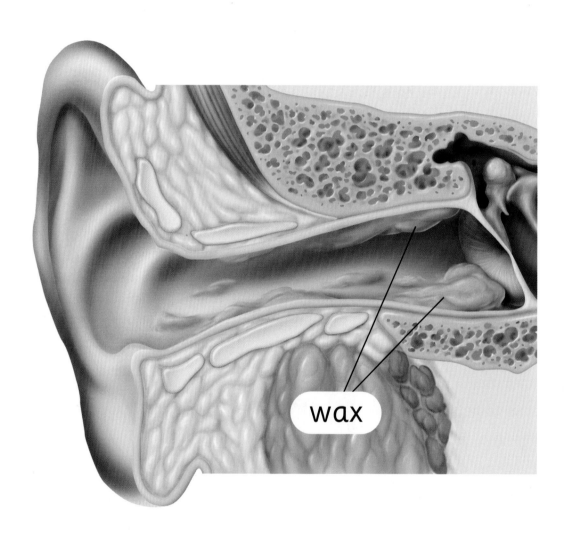

wax

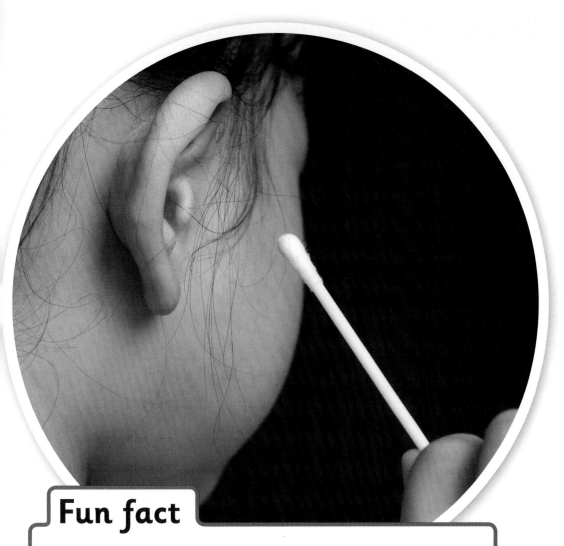

Fun fact

Do not stick cotton buds in ears.
The wax will come out by itself.

Lots of things can help if you cannot hear well.

In the ear

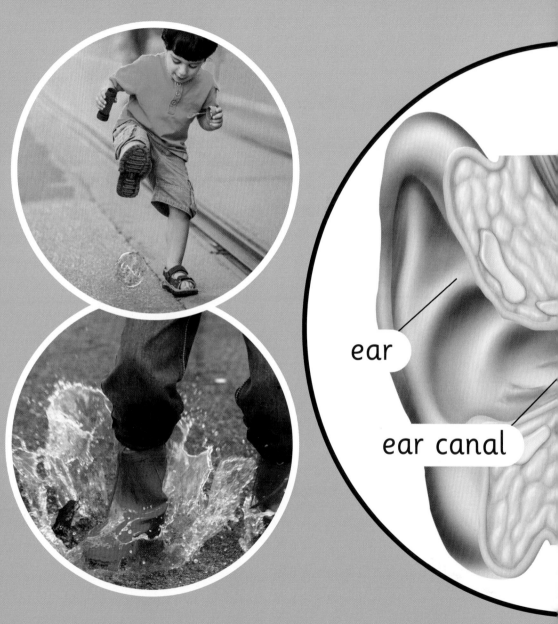

ear

ear canal

wax

eardrum

15

Letters and Sounds: Phase 4

Word count: 100

Focus on adjacent consonants with short vowel phonemes, e.g. /s/ /t/ /a/ /m/ /p/

Common exception words: of, to, the, by, are, you, they, have, like, do, come, little, out, what

Curriculum links (EYFS): Understanding the World: the World

Curriculum links (National Curriculum, Year 1): Science: Animals, Including Humans

Early learning goals: Listening and attention: children listen to stories, accurately anticipating key events and respond to what they hear with relevant comments, questions or actions; Understanding: answer 'how' and 'why' questions about their experiences and in response to stories or events; Reading: read and understand simple sentences, use phonic knowledge to decode regular words and read them aloud accurately, demonstrate understanding when talking with others about what they have read.

National Curriculum: learning objectives: Spoken language: listen and respond appropriately to adults and their peers; Reading/Word reading: apply phonic knowledge and skills as the route to decode words, read aloud accurately books that are consistent with their developing phonic knowledge and that do not require them to use other strategies to work out words; Reading/comprehension: understand both the books they can already read accurately and fluently and those they listen to by drawing on what they already know or on background information and vocabulary provided by the teacher

Developing fluency

- Your child may enjoy hearing you read the book.
- You may wish to read alternate pages, encouraging your child to read with expression those sentences followed by an exclamation mark.

Phonic practice

- Practise reading words that contain adjacent consonants. Model sounding out the following word, saying each of the sounds quickly and clearly. Then blend the sounds together.

  f/a/c/t

- Ask your child to say each of the sounds in the following words. Now ask them to blend the sounds together.

  stamp   scrunch   splat